AF266307

Learning to Live

poems on loss, healing, and becoming whole

by Stacy Huddleston

Published by Bedrock Heritage Publishing

ISBN: 978-1-972179-00-0 (Paper Back)

ISBN: 978-1-972179-05-5 (Hard Cover)

ISBN: 978-1-972179-79-6 (EPUB)

First Edition 2026

This is a work of poetry. Any resemblance to specific persons or events is coincidental or presented as personal reflection.

Printed in the United States of America

For my husband, Bruce,
who stood beside me
as I learned to live.

Acknowledgments

I did not write this book surrounded by many voices.

I acknowledge my husband, Bruce, whose steady presence gave me the space to do the work these pages hold. He stood beside me as I learned to find my own voice and live inside it without fear.

This book was written in solitude, but not without witness.

Contents

Opening Note

This book is not a story of arrival.

It was written in the middle of learning how to live, not after everything was understood. The poems do not move in a straight line because living does not. Some moments repeat, some questions return, and some truths take time to be spoken without fear.

What you will read is not a record of healing as a single turning point, but of many small recognitions. The slow understanding that safety can exist, that choice can exist, and that a person can remain themselves without disappearing for the sake of survival.

There are places in these pages where nothing resolves. That is intentional. Much of life is lived without clear conclusions, and these poems honor the work of staying present even when certainty does not come.

If you find yourself in these words, take what feels true and leave what does not. This book does not ask you to relive anything, only to notice what it means to keep living.

This is a record of learning, not finishing.

A Place Where Trust Broke

A Face Among the Many

I move through rooms
as a face among the many,
recognized only for usefulness

I listen
I nod
I hold what spills from others
and set it gently back inside them

My name is spoken
only when something is needed

My silence is assumed to be ignorance,
but it is the strength that holds me

I am not loud enough
to interrupt the world
not fragile enough
to be noticed

I stand in the narrow space
between capable and invisible

Not seen
Not heard

I ask the quiet question
that has learned to survive
without an answer

Do I matter

Is It My Fault

Is it my fault
that I learned to shrink
instead of being protected

What should I have done
spoken sooner
spoken louder
spoken at all

No one tells you
what to do
when safety never comes

No one protects me

I do not know
how to protect myself
without disappearing

I replay the moments
like there was a correct answer
and I missed it

I was not reckless
I was not careless
I was unguarded
and alone

So I turn inward
not to hide
but because there is nowhere else

I live inside myself now

This Is the Reason Why

This is the reason why
I do not reach for help
until my hands are empty

This is the reason why
I pause before speaking
and often choose not to

This is the reason why
I learned to read rooms
instead of trusting them

When no one protects you
you stop expecting protection
and call it maturity

You learn that needing
does not guarantee care
and silence feels safer
than disappointment

This is the reason why
I hide inside myself
not out of fear
but experience

I have learned
that visibility does not equal safety
and being seen
can still mean being alone

So I keep my strength quiet
my questions contained

my heart behind a door
I built to survive

This is not weakness.
This is adaptation

What Is a Friend

What is a friend
I have never found one

People tell me
who I am
as if they discovered it
without looking

They speak
and I become
whatever fits their sentence

No one asks
what it feels like inside me
what I carry quietly
what I am afraid to name

They assume familiarity
because they stand close
but closeness is not curiosity

I have been described
more than I have been known

I listen
I hold
I make space

Still, no one says
tell me
who you are

So I wonder
if a friend is someone
who pauses long enough
to ask

and stays
long enough
to hear the answer

Why Do I Stay

They tell me
I am not the one

They say it gently,
as if honesty makes it kind

They stay anyway,
using my presence
like a waiting room
until the right life arrives

I give
because I know how,
because being needed
feels like proof

They take
without cruelty,
which somehow hurts more

I ask myself
why do I stay,
as if there is a noble reason

Is attention better than respect
when respect has never chosen me

Is being wanted temporarily
better than being unseen entirely

I stay because leaving
would mean admitting
how little I was asked to matter

I stay
and call it good enough
so I do not have to call it
forgotten

Snake on the Roadside

I thought he was the one

He stood still enough
to look safe,
quiet enough
to seem chosen

I mistook stillness
for sincerity

He was a snake on the roadside,
not chasing,
not warning,
waiting

Waiting for trust
to lower its guard

The poison was not sudden.
It was deliberate.
Measured
Intimate

A new level of cruelty,
the kind that does not shout,
only enters
and spreads

My soul sinks,
then cracks,
then breaks
in stages,

so slow I almost believe
I am surviving it

I walk away altered,
not bleeding where it shows,
carrying the ache
of having believed the dream

when it was a nightmare,
a moral warning I saw
but chose to ignore
for a chance to be loved,
to be seen

After

Everything looked the same,
and the world continued
as if nothing had shifted

I waited for something to stop
a sound,
a movement,
the day itself
anything that would admit
what had happened

Nothing did

I spoke
and heard a stranger
using my voice

The part of me
that trusted and hoped
was gone,
and what remained
could not reach for light

I stood inside my body
and made less of myself,
unsure whether it kept me alive
or was a kind of punishment

I question
every warmth,
every promise
that feels easy

My instincts sit
like startled animals,
alert,
uncertain
which direction is safe

I move carefully now,
as if love
has teeth

The World He Left Behind

He built a dark world around me
slowly,
so I thought it was weather,
not design

Although he is gone,
I live in it

The walls are made of doubt,
the air thick with questions
that keep asking my name

Do I deserve this
as if pain is earned

Do I know how to get out
when the exits were never shown

Will anyone help me
when I have learned
not to expect rescue

I move through this place
carefully,
carrying the blame
he planted
as if it were my own

Some nights I forget
there was ever another sky

Questions I Was Never Meant to Carry

Do I deserve this
as if pain is a sentence
handed down at birth

Is this why I was created
to endure
to absorb
to disappear quietly

Was I made
only to be tested
only to be used
only to survive what others do

I ask the sky
questions it does not answer

Is there hope for me
when hope feels like a language
I was never taught

I stand here
still breathing
still asking

Which must mean
something in me
does not believe
this is the end

Still

I have walked through questions
that had no mercy

I have lived inside doubts
that learned my name

I have wondered
if pain was my purpose
if endurance was all
I was meant to offer

I have waited for answers
that never came
and help
that did not know how to find me

And still

I stand here,
still breathing,
still asking,
still hoping

The Weight of Staying

I carry sorrow
like a thick, wet blanket,
heavy enough
to change how I breathe

There are arrows lodged in my heart,
not all from one wound,
but from many moments
that never healed cleanly

I watch good people leave
too early,
their lives cut short
mid sentence,
mid kindness

And I am still here

I ask the question
no one answers honestly

Is it true
only the good die young,
or is that just a story
we tell
to make sense
of unbearable math

I do not feel spared.
I feel chosen
to carry witness

To remain
with the weight,
with the remembering,
with the ache of staying
when others did not get to

If goodness is measured by leaving,
then what is the meaning
of those who remain

still breathing,
still loving,
still hurting,
still here

Tommy's Chair

I think of Tommy,
the beautiful little boy
who lit up rooms
without trying

Everyone loved him.
Everyone smiled
when he entered,
as if joy recognized itself

His family adored him
He was held
by so many hands,
so many futures imagined
at once

And then he was taken

I sat there
staring at his empty chair,
a shape that felt louder
than any sound

And the question came,
uninvited and merciless

Why am I here
when he is gone

Why does breath stay
in some bodies
and leave others
who were so clearly wanted

There is no math
that makes this fair

There is no answer
that does not break
under the weight
of a child's absence

All I know
is that love does not disappear
just because the chair is empty,
and grief is what remains
when joy had nowhere to go

I am here
asking the question
because I witnessed him,
because I loved him,
because loss leaves echoes
in those who stay

Learning Safety

Testing the Light

I snuck out of the darkness
quietly,
as if it might notice
and pull me back

I stood at the edge
of something brighter
and waited
for it to prove itself

Is this really light,
or just another illusion
that knows how to glow

Is this really my chance,
or a pause
before the fall

I blinked,
half expecting pain,
half expecting relief

I asked the questions
that come
when hope feels unfamiliar

Is this a nightmare
wearing new clothes

Can I escape
without paying for it later

I did not run forward.
I did not turn back

The light stayed by my side.
It did not rush me.
It did not disappear
when I hesitated

It strengthened me
in small, quiet ways
It helped me
stand where I was

I want to believe

Learning the Light

The light began to test me,
not with demands,
but with choices
I had forgotten I was allowed to make

It asked nothing dramatic.
Only this,
do you want to stay,
or do you want to step forward

I was not pushed.
I was not punished
for hesitating

Each small decision
returned something to me
I thought I had lost

My voice.
My direction.
My right to choose

I began to believe
there was a place for me,
not because I proved myself,
but because I was already standing there

The light did not promise safety
It offered space

And for the first time,
that felt like enough

Testing the Light, Again

I had to test the light

I needed to know
it would stay
without holding me captive

I needed to know
I could pause,
pull back,
choose myself
without punishment

I needed to know
that I was in control
of my steps,
that the light
was not another hand
deciding for me

I felt guilty.
I felt ashamed

As if caution were a flaw
instead of wisdom learned
the hard way

But I tested the light
for my own protection,
so it would not turn dark
the moment I trusted it

I watched closely.
I waited

And the light did not threaten.
It did not withdraw.
It did not change its face

It stayed
without asking me
to surrender myself

That is how I know
this light is different

Releasing the Shame

I am letting go
of the shame
for needing to test the light

Caution was not cruelty
It was memory

I did not doubt because I wanted to.
I doubted because I had learned
that brightness can lie,
that warmth can turn,
that silence can sharpen

I was not trying to control the light.
I was trying to keep myself

I carried guilt
as if discernment were betrayal,
as if protecting my heart
meant I was broken

But shame does not belong
to the one who learned slowly

It belongs nowhere now

I tested the light
because I wanted it to stay true.
Because I wanted to believe
without losing myself again

The light did not punish me
for needing proof

And neither will I

I release the idea
that healing must be immediate,
that trust must be blind,
that survival requires apology

I am allowed
to be careful.
I am allowed
to take my time

This is not damage.
This is wisdom
learning how to rest

Letting the Light Come Closer

The light confuses me

It is gentle
where I learned to brace,
steady
where I learned to watch for turns

It is something brand new,
and my body does not yet
have language for it

I say,
will you marry me

and then,
I will never marry you

as if I am testing
whether I am allowed
to want
and refuse
in the same breath

I feel cruel
I feel mean

But I am not trying to wound.
I am trying to see
if I can choose
without losing myself

I long for the light,
for strength,
for stability,

but my hands still remember
what it cost
to reach too quickly

So I pull close
and push away,
not to confuse him,
but to steady me

This is what it looks like
when desire meets fear
and neither is lying

I am not rejecting the light.
I am learning
how near it can come
without burning me

And that distance,
for now,
is mine to decide

A Place to Run

I am searching for a place,
somewhere I can run
without rehearsing an escape

With him,
I can stop hiding,
set down the vigilance
that never learned how to sleep

And still, I am afraid
that if I rest too fully,
I will lose myself
inside the safety I have never known

So I pull him close,
then push him away,
my body arguing
with what my heart already wants

I am not testing his devotion
I am testing the ground

I want him near,
not consuming,
not leaving,
just present

I want him to hold me firmly,
the way you hold something precious,
not to restrain,
but to steady

I want to be hugged
without disappearing,
held
without being owned

I want him to say,
you are safe,
and for my body
to believe it

I have never been safe

So this reaching
and retreating
is not rejection

It is the slow work
of learning
how to stay
without losing myself

Learning Safety

I am learning
what safety feels like,
not as an idea,
but as something lived
inside my body

It is quieter
than I expected

No urgency
No chasing
No needing to prove
my worth to stay

Safety does not rush me
It does not test me
It does not disappear
when I speak my fear aloud

I am learning
what it is
to be in a relationship
where my nervous system
is allowed to rest

Where closeness
does not require surrender
Where space
does not mean abandonment

I am learning
that love can be steady
without being dull,
strong
without being sharp

I practice saying
this is too much,
and hearing
that's okay

I practice staying
when nothing is wrong,
when there is no crisis
to anchor us together

This is new
This is slow

I am learning
that safety is not perfection,
but consistency

Not intensity,
but care that returns

And maybe
this is what it means
to be with someone,
not as armor,
not as rescue,
but as two people
choosing to remain
present,
kind,
and real

When Fear Returns

Sometimes fear arrives
without an invitation,
like an old curtain
pulled across the room

An argument,
a look,
and all those feelings
rush back at once,
too fast to sort

The past does not knock.
It floods

I do not know what to do
with my body
when memory takes over

He becomes quiet.
I become loud

Not because we want to hurt,
but because we are reaching
in opposite directions
for safety

His silence feels like distance
My voice feels like urgency

We miss each other
by inches,
by timing,
by fear speaking first

I am not trying to fight.
I am trying to be found

He is not trying to leave.
He is trying not to make it worse

And in that space,
where neither of us is wrong,
I am learning
to pause,
to breathe,
to remember
this moment is not the past
even when it feels like it

Why I Run

I retreat to my room
and hide again,
not because I want distance,
but because my thoughts need quiet
before they turn sharp

I want to repair.
I just need time
to find my words
without shouting them

I wonder
how to make my needs known
without becoming loud,
how to ask for closeness
without pushing it away

I sit with the questions
until my body softens enough
to think

He checks on me

Not urgently
Not accusing
Just there

And my heart flutters,
a small, startled relief

I know he is still here
I know he still cares

He is not leaving me

So why do I do this
why do I run
as if safety needs chasing
or distance proves something

I run because hiding
once kept me safe

I run because staying
used to cost too much

And now I am learning
that retreat does not have to mean goodbye,
that silence can be a pause,
not an ending

I come back slowly,
not because I am chased,
but because I am wanted
without pressure

That is new

And maybe that is why
I am still learning
how to stay

Returning to Myself

Learning Balance

I need to find balance,
a place that does not tip
too far into needing
or too far into doing it alone

I love how he tries
to fix things for me,
to smooth the sharp edges
when I am overwhelmed

There is comfort
in being steadied,
in knowing someone sees
the weight
before I collapse under it

And still,
I want to stand on my own

I want my feet to remember
their strength,
my hands to trust
they can hold
what is mine to carry

I do not want to disappear
into being cared for,
or prove my worth
by refusing help

I want to lean
without falling

I want him to fix things
when the world is too loud,
and to step back
when I find my ground again

I want partnership,
not rescue

I am learning
that balance is not choosing
between independence and support,
but letting them take turns

Some days I walk beside him.
Some days I pause
and let him steady me

And some days,
the bravest thing I do
is say,
I can handle this,
and also,
I need you here

Becoming

I never thought
I could dream

I never thought
I would be anything
more than what I survived

Wanting felt indulgent.
Hoping felt dangerous

And then he stood beside me,
not carrying me,
but steadying the ground
long enough
for me to look up

When my strength thinned,
when doubt spoke louder
than possibility,
he pointed toward the horizon
and said,
go

He believed
on the days
I could not

He reminded me
that fear is not truth,
that hesitation is not failure,
that dreams do not belong
only to the fearless

Now I am moving
toward something
I once thought
was not meant for me

And I am amazed,
not because he pushed me forward,
but because I walked

I do not recognize myself,
and yet
this version feels
more honest
than the one who never tried

I am becoming
someone who dreams
without apologizing,
someone who reaches
without disappearing

And that
is the miracle
I am still learning
to believe

Where We Landed

I recognize
how he has been there for me,
and how I have been there for him,
not perfectly,
but faithfully

He wanted to move to the South.
He did not know
it was the dream
I carried quietly
since childhood

No declarations
No bargaining
Just two paths
leaning toward the same horizon
without realizing it

And now,
here we are

He is where he wants to be.
I am where I want to be

Not by accident.
Not by force
But by a series of yeses
spoken at the right time
to the right life

I look around
and feel it settle in my chest

This is amazing
This is a blessing

Not loud.
Not flashy
Just right

More than I dared to dream.
More than I knew
how to imagine

Something aligned.
Something kind

And for once,
I do not question it

Before We Knew

We talk about when we were younger
and it feels
like we were moving around each other
without knowing the pattern

We crossed paths
more than once,
two lives passing close
without recognition

We lived in the same hours,
walked through the same seasons,
stood in the same places
and kept going

We brushed the edges
of the same world,
near enough to meet,
not yet ready to see

Other things filled our lives then,
lessons not yet learned,
roads that had to finish
before this one could begin

It is as if life was making room,
quietly removing
what could not remain,
waiting for the moment
we could stay

Sometimes it feels like chance,
the way timing softened,

the way our steps aligned
without effort

Sometimes it feels like God,
patient and unseen,
guiding without explanation,
trusting we would arrive
when we were able

We did not miss each other.
We were becoming

And when we finally met,
it felt less like beginning
and more like recognition,
as if something long forming
had finally spoken

The Girl in the Closet

I grieve the little girl
hidden in the closet,
knees pulled tight,
breath held
so the world would not hear her exist

She learned early
that quiet could be armor,
that stillness might be mercy

No one told her
she was allowed to take up space

I find her there still,
curled around hope
like something fragile
she was not sure
she was meant to keep

I want her to know
she is safe now

That the door is open.
That the house is warm
That no one is waiting
to punish her for being seen

I want her to know
she is wanted,
not for what she provides
not for how small she can make herself,
but simply because she is here

I want her to know
she is loved
without condition,
without cost,
without fear of being taken away

I want her to know
she is full of possibilities,
that her life was never meant
to stay folded in the dark,
that dreams were always hers,
even when no one said so

I kneel beside her now
and whisper
you do not have to hide anymore

I am here.
I will stay.
And together,
we will learn
what it means
to live in the light

Teaching Her to Dream

I hold the little girl
as she steps out of the closet,
blinking at the light
as if it might change its mind

I tell her
she can dream now

Her dreams spill out softly,
a southern home
with wide porches and slow evenings,
a beautiful ball gown
that lets her feel chosen,
a white picket fence
that promises steadiness and peace

I listen
without correcting her.
Without laughing
Without taking anything away

I tell her
it is safe to dream

But I also tell her
we will not live there

Dreams are not shelter
They are not plans
They are not where life happens

Imagination opens doors,
but it is not the room
we stay in

Life is lived
in imperfect houses,
in borrowed courage,
in choices made
while fear still whispers

I tell her
we can want beauty
without waiting for it to save us

We can love softness
without disappearing into it

I take her hand
and show her the world
where breath is real,
where footsteps matter,
where joy is built
one honest moment at a time

Dreams may visit us,
but living
is how we stay

What She Deserved

I let her know
that she is seen,
not glanced at,
not imagined,
but truly seen

I let her know
that she is loved,
not for surviving,
not for being quiet,
not for enduring,
but simply because she exists

I tell her
what no one told her then

What happened to you
was not your fault

You did not invite it
You did not cause it
You did not deserve it

I tell her
that children are meant
to be cherished,
to be protected,
to be held
when the world feels too large

She deserved gentleness
She deserved safety.
She deserved someone
to stand between her
and harm

I tell her
the truth
until it settles
into her bones

You were never wrong
for wanting love

You were never weak
for needing protection

You deserved to be cared for,
fully,
fiercely,
without condition

I hold her
until she stops bracing,
until her breath
learns a new rhythm

And I promise her this,
the part I can keep now

I see you.
I love you.
I will protect you

You are safe with me

The Promise I Keep

I kneel to her height
so she does not have to look up
to be heard

I tell her
you are safe with me

Not because the world is gentle,
but because I will not abandon you
inside it

I tell her
I will uphold you
when your legs shake,
when your voice wavers,
when fear tries to make your choices
for you

I tell her
I will respect you,
your no,
your slowness,
your need to pause,
your right to take up space
without earning it

I tell her
I will cherish you,
not for what you become,
not for what you give,
but for who you already are

I will not rush you
toward healing.
I will not silence you
for comfort

I will not ask you
to be brave
before you are ready

I place my hands
where protection should have been
and I stay

This is not a dream.
This is a vow

And this time,
it is kept.

Where Life is Lived

Moral Injury

Moral injury is hard

It is the ache that comes
not from what you wanted,
but from what you endured
when wanting was not safe

I did not choose this for myself
I need to say that
without arguing with it

And still,
I let it happen,
not because I agreed,
but because I was trying
to survive inside choices
that were already broken

This is where the pain lives,
between blame and truth,
between what I value
and what fear required of me

I replay the moment
as if clarity had been available,
as if strength had been evenly distributed,
as if I was not already wounded
before the choice appeared

I ask myself
how do I feel okay about myself now
when my own conscience
feels bruised and tender

I start here.

I stop calling adaptation
a failure of character

I stop demanding purity
from a version of me
who only knew how to endure

I learn to sit
with what happened
without sentencing myself for it

Letting go does not mean forgetting.
It does not mean approving

It means loosening the grip
of the voice that says
you are forever defined
by your most powerless moment

I let go in pieces

I let go of the belief
that pain is proof of who I am

I let go of the fantasy
that I could have escaped
unchanged

What I keep
is the value that was violated
The part of me that knew
this was not right

That part is not broken
It is alive

And maybe healing
is not becoming innocent again,
but becoming aligned,
slowly,
gently,
now

I am not absolving myself
I am reclaiming myself

And that
is how I begin
to feel okay
enough
to live

What I Release

I see now
that there are many kinds of wounds,
many kinds of fear

Some people knew
exactly what they were doing

What they did
was on purpose

It came from fear
It came from pain
From places in them
that were never healed

That truth does not excuse it
It explains it

I forgive them
not to clear their names,
not to rewrite what happened,
but to loosen
the grip they once had on me

I do not carry their fear anymore
I do not rehearse their choices
as if they were mine to answer for

I leave what belongs to them
where it belongs

Forgiveness, for me,
is not reconciliation
It is release

And I am free enough
to set this down now

Learning to Forgive Myself

Forgiving myself
is slower

I keep meeting
the version of me
who did not know
what I know now

She made choices
with limited light,
with a nervous system
trained to survive

I have wanted
to punish her
for not seeing sooner,
for hoping too long,
for staying when leaving
felt impossible

But punishment
has never been healing

I am not living in the past
I am clear about that

And still,
sometimes the past creeps in,
soft footed,
unannounced,
asking to be acknowledged
one more time

I do not panic anymore.
I do not disappear

I notice it
I breathe.
I remind myself
where I am

This moment is different
I am different

Forgiving myself
does not mean forgetting.
It means refusing
to keep sentencing
the person I used to be

I am allowed
to grow
without dragging guilt
behind me

I offer myself
the patience
I once gave everyone else

And slowly,
that is enough

Time at Rest

I am learning
to rest in time,
not rushing forward,
not dragging the past behind me

I see now
that there are many kinds of hardship,
many kinds of wounds

Some people know
exactly what they are doing

What they did
was on purpose

And still,
it came from fear,
from pain,
from places in them
that were never healed

That truth does not excuse it
It explains it

I forgive them

Not loudly
Not ceremonially
Just enough
to loosen the hold
they once had on me

Forgiving myself
is slower

I am still learning
how to release the version of me
who did not know
what I know now

I am not living in the past
I am clear about that

And still,
sometimes the past creeps in,
soft footed,
unannounced,
asking to be acknowledged
one more time

I do not panic anymore
I do not disappear

I notice it
I breathe
I remind myself
where I am

This moment is different
I am different

Time does not demand perfection
It asks for presence

And so I rest here,
forgiving what I can,
learning what I must,

allowing the past
to pass through
without becoming my home

What I Protect

Life has been hard,
the school of hard knocks,
and I have learned

I have learned
what is valuable
and what is worth protecting

I protect my marriage
I protect my time
I protect my space

Not because I am afraid,
but because these things
hold my life together

I make my choices
with eyes open now

I no longer drift
into decisions
hoping they will save me

I choose,
and I stand
within the consequences
of those choices

I do not outsource my life
I do not wait for permission

Because these choices are mine
I made them for myself

And that is not selfish
That is sovereignty

The Work I Chose

I promised myself
I will not fail,
not because failure is forbidden,
but because I will keep showing up
even when I tremble

I chose the hard work

The kind that asks
for honesty,
for patience,
for staying
when leaving would be easier

Through blood, sweat, and tears,
not as a saying,
but as a lived truth,
I built something real

My dream came true,
not because it was easy,
not because the path was clear,
but because I grew strong enough
to walk it anyway

Strength did not arrive suddenly
It was made
in quiet decisions,
in boundaries held,
in choosing myself
again and again

And I did not do it alone

He walks with me,
not in front of me,
not carrying me,
but beside me,
steady and present

Together,
we stand in what was earned,
not borrowed,
not imagined,
but lived

This is not luck.
This is not rescue

This is the result
of the strength I built
and the love
that stayed

What I Carry Forward

I have learned
that my pain has purpose,
not because it was meant to happen,
but because it did

I have learned
that what comforted me
can now pass through my hands
to others

I can sit with grief
without trying to fix it
I can listen
without turning away

I can validate pain
without needing to soften it,
without rushing anyone
toward meaning before they are ready

I know the weight
of unanswered questions
I know the dark
that convinces you
there is no way out

And because I know it,
I can point gently
toward the light,
not as rescue,
but as possibility

I remember
what happened to me

I do not deny it
I do not relive it

I carry it
as knowledge,
as depth,
as steadiness earned

What tried to break me
now strengthens my hands

I will use what I have learned
to uphold others,
to stand beside them
when the path is unclear,
to remind them
they are not alone

This is not sacrifice
This is continuity

Pain did not get the final word.
Purpose did

Choosing the Field

I have walked through the fire.
I have crawled on my knees
when standing felt impossible

I have learned
not to place my life
in other people's hands,
not because love is dangerous,
but because my life is mine
to tend

I have learned
that I have choices,
even when they are small,
even when they cost me comfort,
even when they ask more of me
than I thought I had

I am grounded in hope now,
not the fragile kind,
but the kind that grows
from truth
and keeps its feet on the ground

I am still learning
to trust myself,
to listen when my body speaks,
to believe my knowing
without waiting for permission

I am choosing
to live this life,

not observe it,
not postpone it,
not sit quietly on the sidelines
waiting to be called in

I step forward
with what I have learned,
with what I carry,
with who I am becoming

I am here.
I choose this life

Finding Gratitude

I am learning
to find gratitude on purpose,
to set my mind
toward noticing
what is already here

Not because life is easy,
but because it is happening
whether I pay attention
or not

I look for it
in simple things

The breath that returns
without being asked
Light moving across the day
Nature doing what it does
without urgency

I notice it
in relationships,
in the way presence
sometimes says more
than words

I make room
for both,
the challenges
that shape me
and the quiet joys

that surprise me
when I am not looking for them

I learn to savor
a moment
instead of rushing past it
toward the next one

To stay
long enough
to feel satisfied
with what this day offers,
with the opportunities
and experiences
that are shaping
who I am becoming

Gratitude, for me,
is not pretending

It is choosing
to see clearly,
to honor what is real,
and to let the ordinary
be enough

Learning to Be on My Own Side

I am learning
to love myself
not loudly,
not perfectly,
but consistently

I am learning
to be my greatest encourager,
the voice that says
keep going
without demanding more
than today can give

I am learning
to be my own best friend,
to speak to myself
with patience,
to notice when I am tired
instead of pushing through it

I can self correct now,
not with punishment,
but with honesty

I can pause and ask,
what do I need
in this moment,
what would make this day
a little kinder

I am learning
to look for opportunity

not only in ambition,
but in ordinary joy

A quiet morning.
A shared laugh.
A breath that feels easy

I am learning
that happiness is not a destination,
it is attention

It is allowing myself
to be where I am
without wishing myself elsewhere

This is not settling.
This is presence

And each day,
I choose to stand with myself,
to enjoy the life I am living,
to meet it with openness
instead of expectation

I Am Enough

I am enough.

Not because I proved it,
not because I earned it,
but because I am here,
whole and breathing

I am worthy of love
and respect,
not as a reward,
but as a given

There is nothing
I cannot work toward,
nothing I cannot learn,
nothing beyond reach
when I stand in my own life

I am choosing my path,
not the one fear outlined,
not the one handed to me,
but the one that feels honest
under my feet

I am living my life now,
present,
imperfect,
awake

And if you are reading this,
paused at the edge
of your own becoming,
hear me say it clearly.

Live your life

Not later.
Not when you are braver.
Not when you are healed enough.

Now.

Closing Thoughts

Some things healed slowly.
Some questions never resolved.

What changed most
was my willingness to keep living
inside the days I was given.

If you recognized yourself anywhere here,
you were never asked to carry it alone.

Take what was useful.
Leave what was not.

Living is not a finish line.
It is something we practice.

And life goes on.